The Dark Heart

Also by Sarah Tiffen and published by Ginninderra Press
Learning Country
Mythica
The Light Breaks Open

Sarah Tiffen

The Dark Heart

The Dark Heart
ISBN 978 1 76041 011 7
Copyright © text Sarah Tiffen 2015

First published 2015 by
GINNINDERRA PRESS
PO Box 3461 Port Adelaide SA 5015
www.ginninderrapress.com.au

Contents

I	7
To the Opal Miner	9
Autism Spectrum Innumeratum	12
Condoleeza's Price	16
Srebenica	17
Firestorm	18
Extremis	23
II	25
Survival	27
Storm Haiku	29
The Winter Cometh	30
Tilley's, Thursday night, Winter	32
Back Mountain Country	34
The Yellow Man: Winter in the Capital	36
One Afternoon in Solitude	38
The Watchful Night	39
III	41
Frogs: Ecology of Hope	43
Bees	46
Catholic Schoolyard	47
Seahorse Memory	49
fireflies	50
IV	51
Diagnos	53
Fallen Small	54
Boundary Web	55
Trying Not To Die	56
Witness	58
The Tilleys Papers	60

V   65
Meeting Les Murray   67
For Gerard Manley Hopkins   72
For Judith Wright   74
For Kenneth Slessor – Five Bells   76
For Seamus Heaney   78
For Walt Whitman   80
For Emily Dickinson   81

VI   83
Totem   85
The Departed   86
The Sewing Room   87
Wedding Day   88

VII   91
My Dark Heart   93
Woman   95
First Blood   96
Just One   97
Poem about Love   98
Walking Wild Side   100
Where Did the Bad Man Touch You?   101

I

To the Opal Miner

In the back country
Uncle Barney, glistering out of the gloom,
tall and barnacled,
the jut of his jaw like an anvil,
mantled brow. His skin
red-freckled from years on the road, from
out-of-place-ness –
the face all cheekbone
eyebrows and chin
hands elkhorn busy and wry.

He wore worn woollen and spoke from a small
fissure at the side of his face. He spread
wide the orange garment of his arms and knelt in dirt,
before the altar of last night's bonfire, all
concertinaed and felt-mettled, his fingers tooled the coals
fingered them around, worked the
white flesh of flour and water pressed to a wad.
With the heel of his black miner's boot he made a hole in the ash
and with the heel of his hand he pressed the cloudy dough
and made a dent and there – he slipped it underground
dent to dent in
ashes filmy eyelash, coals evicted from the seams of wood.

We ate what he later picked out, plucked from fire to prising –
soft yellowish cake of
that bush bread. Uncovered. Damper.

This man spent lost years in far places
underground scratching and working the earth away,
excavating small-ly buried sky – the sunlight blue sea
   condensed spectra-
blue opal plucked from red dirt like plums from fat pudding and
fingered, turned and pocketed.
He turned them over and again, eyed them like
eyeing a woman, the yearning and need and
pleasure in the form then
brought them to us in a small bag
which he held up and watched me watching, from his opal-
   fragment eye.

I liked his angled distance
as I looked up from country
to a depth of angled man
and felt the quietness of him.
Framed against opal sky
smoke twisting from coals
That fierce erotic blue
pressed against stars in the
dark curtain of night.
He pocketed himself there and silent.
That Tall Unspeaking Uncle
folded now into the black swag of sky
where the silence is most complete.

And we hold within the recess of ourselves-
the scent of damper in winter
the small exhale of childish breath as we ate,
the vapour on the air.
The opal of it weighed on the tongue like a stone.

Autism Spectrum Innumeratum

for Daniel Tammet

The boy opened his eyes to the world.
Born on a blue day

emerging from his cawl
beaky-eyed and hungry
blinked in the fishbowl world
the swimming ocean at him:
sea of spiky numbers, bright and curled.

*

He gulped the numbers outside air
hungry upside down and flapping fish
lapping, hung in sky, the
rivulets and tides across his mind,
he ate the numbers with his eyes –
they stroked and tasselled on his brain
his gobbling wish

shapes made a hieroglyph of sound beneath his
tongue and crawled his skin like
dragonflies, chasing chime
painting up his cavities and in his throat
and scraping, crackling, cackling in
his ribs, his solar plexus
colour calculus sublime.

*

sometimes textures
spectrum sibelian
streamed from out his mind
aurora borealis, wise reptilian

*

N...n...n...n...n numbers
yawped his yelping heart
Numbers! Numbers! Numbers!
Numb with fear he felt their flight-
sharp and angular as gas
pricking him and salving him with shapes
his window and his light.

*

And..
when...
he...
closed his eyes
he saw dancing
algorithmia
mesmerical numerical symphonia
logical topography
graphic of the great mathematic,
O Pi-ous one.

*

And…
when…
he…
spake he spake
in primes and composites and
went kingly through the
landscape of Pi to 22 514 –
Absolutely Pitch-Perfect Enormous
benumbered sky.

*

And what they saw
inside his flawless head – amazed.
A map – into Infinity…
only for him, the undistracted rapture
of a numbered scripture.

*

Later, the structures grew linguistic
He learned Icelandic to himself
in seven days
like the creation of the world
the joy unfurled
and on the seventh day he spoke like a native
and he didn't rest.

*

They thought – he's different
He knows numbers but – he can't learn Human,
never will
but still – even
that language rose from deep
inside the mist, within the numbers, did exist.

He came to love and give
how cautiously and generously
and told us how he lives,
and through this,
he sees us, and he forgives.

Condoleeza's Price

Fallujah is in ruins.
The Black Sorceress and her Jester collude
in the Cathedral of the Five Lies.
When she smiles, the axe mark of
concentration camps deeper in her brow.
She is a study of servitude. Capable of evil.
Her womb is empty – no mother would commit her sins.
In broken mosques the bodies of children burn.
And in the churches of Westminster,
Washington, Baghdad, mothers, daughters and wives
mourn the passing of men, the passing of meaning.

Srebenica

White columns in silent geometry
Across a lawn as wide as mountains:
A quiet that is never peaceful
The shudder of meaning exhumed and renounced.
No monument, however stark,
Can make sense of that
Still day, when 8,000
Brown-eyed boys and men
Walked away to the forest
Looked in the eye by brothers
And slain one by one
Until the silence was a
Deafening scalding roar.

Blood, blood…
And women mouthing silent shock,
Their hands still warm from last goodbyes.
Son, husband, brother, father…
And still, with years entombing that ferocious sacrilege,
The fearful keening, and still the screams of fear,
The swallowed heart, the broken and unanswered why?

Firestorm

In memoriam – Black Saturday, the Year of Our Lord 2009

I Paradise Found

It's cool in the forest:
tangled bark peels from the
mountain ash like tall cool
women shedding their clothes
arrested in rangy intimacy
their stately undress mile upon
mile of still white trees
thronging with still bracken at their feet.

II Dreaming

We walked in the
Big Tree Forest, all crackly stringy
and the hum of creatures in
the curly ferns and bracken
and all around up to the sky
little bells in the bell forest
like a heartbeat pulsing gently
'Gently, gently,' she said, as we
skipped and stepped soft as moss.
We were so small in there in the
Big Quiet Green, we were small
and the forest was Big
and she said,
'Stop a bit, Blossom,
and look up – look.'

And high as high
I saw from the crackly bracken ground
and 'Shhh,' says Mummy
and I went quiet as quiet
and my eyes went up and up.
Follow the trunk of the smooth white gums
aaaalllllllll the way up and up and it
went forever into sky
that winked above us…
and it was like water in there
and the tallest place in the world
I ever knew.
And like the old ones we were born anew.

III Falling

It was very hot when they awoke,
the air like a dry hot clamp.
Daddy said, 'Little hot bub,'
snuggling in bed.
Mummy rubbed her head and said
'Hey, darling girl' with clouded eyes.
They lay in close
while Daddy went to make the tea.
The air was hot! The air was hot!
And then the story rises to a blur.

I see it now – a little face pressed to the window,
eyes
drinking in the jellied light, green glass
and shimmering,
and birds were panting on the lawn
their beaks awry, poor little birds,
their little tongues…
and we feel
through fingertips
against the pane, a slight trembling,
an even, tremorous feel
and hear the faintest far far away
sound of surf, or liquid sizzling
and brown darkening.
And she held me close then.
Right. Into. Her. Chest.

IV Ceasing and Becoming

It's all there:
The chimes on the veranda gets louder and louder
and the wind like an animal
stirs the bush
then the rushing and the roaring
from nowhere
Something Big coming quickly
and from nowhere.
And the light like a nightmare, all
orange then green
then dark, dark then black.

And outside the wind,
and then in,
then out again,
and someone saying, 'God, O God!'
And. Then. The Quiet…and then
The ROARING LIKE A GREAT MONSTER.

V Angels Fear

Up, up into the sky together
and the big trees
and all joining with the forest and
the birds and the big white trees
and secret forms
all sighing in a great gust
sweeps upward on the wall of massive
burning light and sound
and higher and higher and
SEE the MONSTER BURNING
hungry BURNING eating
eating up the WHOLE. WORLD.

VI Longtime Dreaming

We always walk in the forest
early in the morning – it's
cool there and green and parrots
peppered there their flash of green and blue
like swipes of paint against pale dappling
going back for miles of light and bark.

The trees
and ferns
and trickling of water.
We walk and play there innocent
and secretly; we are
the Luckiest People with our
slice of heaven –
in the Beautiful Place
in the Beautiful Bereft.
Spirits.

And how I watch from high up
where the air is a whisper of light
and I see it all in silence –
its past beauty
its beauty to return…
And we are floating
beyond the fathoms of sky
beyond reckoning..
We are here…always…
in the Burnt Places and
the Budding Places
seeking peace
And haunting, haunting for centuries
while the tears fill rivers with their grief.

AMEN.

Extremis

Three boys, one soldier,
then two boys…
then 600 children dead
and 3,312 children maimed.
Shame.
Shame.
Shame.

II

Survival

Before dawn in the winter dark
The hills are a black frown
And the street lights a bespoke adornment
Of the Icicle Fairies, feyly strung.
Some force draws me from my bed.
Rugged in scarf and hat pulled down, and up.
I will the house to sleep and step out
To the barely acknowledged world
The dark a burka for my new emboldened heart
A thief, assassin – stride I from the warm chrysalis
Into the bracing cold.

I walk as though survival is at stake
At stake – those few dear lives, my faith,
The future of the everything I know,
The world, the dreams of men, and all else.
Houses are dark cats tucked into themselves –
Not one clatter, no stirring, no bright stars,
The winking of no lone lit window, no signs
Of life, but in the subcutaneous burr of many
Sleeping breaths.
I seek the hill.

Each step a brace into some staunch chill
A warning from the crypt, a sign.
My muscles ache and flex.
My breath inside the scarf, so warm familiar,
My pant, my power surge,
The sharp incline through hillside suburbs
As the night relinquishes itself to
Pale grey light and secret fog.

My bones, my earth, my blood.
I cannot say.
Only solitude and sweat.
Only hearty breath.
Only fear, only love.
Each birthing day a requiem
Unto itself, for all that's ever been
For all that's lost, for all that
Cannot be reclaimed.
I cannot say, because the utterance
Would break the heart and banish meaning.
In each nut, each kernel, every blade, each vein, each cell,
And the austere, unbearable beauty of
The world – at that moment when the light ascends –
The grief repeats itself, the grief, the joy
The tremble in my temples.

Courage only will deliver me,
From all that ever was and will remain.
I go inside, returned.
The warm house soughing with ordinary joys.

Storm Haiku

I

The great rainy mountains
Up high looking down on all I see.
A little fire burning.
A shudder of gold amidst grey.
Winter window pane pale with a scarf of breath.

II

Still in the eye of the storm
The cloud pushes over the mountain
grey on grey – the rain falls like a torrent
Watching from the high window, my heart shudders with desire.

The Winter Cometh

On this day, winter comes.
Her grey wool coat, her wuthering dark
He clusters of gold rustling, her lamps,
And firelight, her cryptic cold, her still.
No sunlight, but the glassy grey,
And storms promised.
Pine tree stands sentinel to ancient things
Ancient and steady. I can not but follow.
At the woodpile, leaves gather a papery affray,
Thronging against the trees, the steps, the cracks in the
Cement, the stones and crannies, the huddled crowds.
The wood is hard, heavy and splintered. It smells
Of resin and dirt.
I take up the axe, chop into it – my arms, back and legs
Forming an axe of effort – the hard lunge down,
The clean swipe, the shudder up the spine.
My body pays homage to the menial and manual-
To all those before me.
It is the fibre, texture of earth, wood and stone,
The need for warmth, the homely
Routines of making real
The bones and order of the day.
The winter day. Winter cometh.
Cold as stone, and sturdy.
In my grandmother's cardigan, I
Hang washing in the dull light
Rain is always moments away,
The cold steel of it needling the air.
My children's clothes embody my children.
They are the life and blood of the past and the future.

They are mine. They are themselves.
I hang their clothes and pay homage
To the menial and manual – to all those before me…and beyond.
Who could deny their warm bodies? Their odours. Their
 dirty happy glee?
Their bright and their inimitable strong?

On this day
Winter contracting the sky and
Coming in cold as when all has ceased to be.
In darkling light, the kitchen is a warm workhouse
The Making space. I chop the onions
And they make me cry, their bitter pungent flesh
Their fresh and sharp-
Garlic, carrots, leek, potato, yam.
The poetry of roots and tubers, base metals
To the alchemy of winter food, brewing broth,
The measured, calming timeless routines.
I wash my hands, and wipe my eyes with the tea-towel,
And pay homage to all I have and all who have gone before.
Here's to food and broth, earth and wood and stone,
And to the bodies that carried children
And to the body that strains against the structure and is
 shaped by them.
And prayer to winter
The cold shield against complacency
On my knees I scrub the floor – it is hard
And hurts my knees.
Winter penance
Winter prayer
Winter time.

Tilley's, Thursday night, Winter

Blood-coloured
walls, floors, dark wood, booth, ceiling, fans
blood coloured
lips, hair, shoes, cushions, curtains, wine
blood-coloured
hearts, thoughts, music like a dark liqueur
gold lamps, towering potted palms
windows painted rain
streets outside
wet and slick with winter night
slivers of silver amongst blood-coloured shadows
streetlights blurring into gold
night thoughts – blood-coloured.

People talking, taking, blurring
flurried round the bar and stirring
blood coloured bar, lined up with
glasses, bottles, liquor, chic adorned.
mirrored flaws, massed hydrangeas
full and faded blooms like
faded madams scorned..
pale Parisian girls behind the bar,
their lips blood-coloured
before the crowd, beyond the blur
half a smile, buttoned up and coolly kind
faint arrogance, resigned demur
brass fittings, curtain rings, bar rim, slip rail spur
brickwork, wood and brass, velvet and the burnished glass
hidden wounds, blood-coloured.

Pale Parisian lady, dressed in black,
trim and French, poised, beautiful and sad –
her eyes, large with love and loss,
mascaraed, lined, but regally refined
poised, reserved and quietly defined.
refracted light disperses and congeals
glistening, ardent dark and deep
voluptuous, the past opined.
'en culture', couture, Tilley's – a woman's poem to the world.

Back Mountain Country

(Yarrangobilly, Tumut)

Here in the Back Mountain Country
the moon hangs in its broken doorway between lake and sky.
The silence is profound, deep as a well.
Only stars make themselves heard
in the empty house of night.
Only the mountains watch in austere eminence,
black giants slumbering in cloistered cold.

The lake is a sacred fjord.
It lies in the dark like an omen,
black and still and deeper than death, a silent repeating prayer.
Still as stone, as the furrowed stone brow of the hill
that watches southward,
that shone in the dying sun,
and now speaks ancient words
older than life.

Still, the silence – huge and complete, deep as a well.
The mountain-people are quietened by the landscape.
Beneath them for mile upon mile
Yarrangobilly labyrinths
snaking back to an underground terrestrial womb-
where men are lost, and spirits lie in wait
and echo up the knowledge of that hollow sacred land

And the moon, white with coming winter,
hangs in the broken doorway of the night
like a portal
and here is the waiting amidst frank loneliness,
is the ache,
is God gathering thoughts.

The Yellow Man: Winter in the Capital

the yellow man is walking
by the lake, his pants, his boots, his raincoat and his socks
yellow, dirty yellow, ochre,
pulled-down beanie, brown,
an armour against being seen
but he is:
the yellow man
colour of dirt and building sites in rain, rock-yellow, mustardy
and stained
he is walking with his head down
in slow steps
pushing the curtain of grey
strained against the winterland,
muted, pushing back thoughts
his skin swallows his eyes
the red of weathered wood
premonitions and memories chafed away
by wind scoured blank
numbed and calm in dispossession.

the brand of burning years stubbed out
beneath the boot of cold.

the yellow man is walking
between the water and the shallows of man
the shadows and the mountain,
rock and soil
lake a bevelled mirror
where he can't look.

he always stays
near the paddle boats, hovers
round the bike and ice cream shop
seeing only the skeletons of
trees and stars
I see from afar he carries a sack of stony dignity
on his tired back.

up close
walkers and cyclists smell him
smoke and urine on snow-born winds-
odour of loss
scent of their own shortfalls
and their empty fears
quickly they pass on, and he
he shuffles back and forth between the city and the water
peripheral, archaic, archetype

he
seeks solace in the footpaths,
it seems he doesn't feel the cold
but where does he go at night when
the dark falls like a knife against the
neck of the lonely winter city?

the lights of the citadel parliament
streak the black lake with yellow tears.

One Afternoon in Solitude

(Mithem, July)

One afternoon in solitude.
The sky was a blue tear of silk
Proclaiming the light
As gold as a spill of honey
And the wooden house
Picked up the sunlight
Basking resplendent in rose and gold,
A palette for my senses
As replete and serene as prayer.
The bush hushed and hushed.
The air was crystalline.
Write, walk, sleep, potter in silence
As the fire cracked.
My thoughts like a long broad river
Quiet and solemn.
O Solemn Day. The solemn
Lacquered surface of the dam
So deep, so still
Waiting, calming, ending
In the dove grey twilight
With the mountains bathed in light
And the full moon in a dying sky
Watching like a Buddha, the turning earth.

The Watchful Night

The watchful night.
The complete dark.

And rain on the tin roof
As constant, soft and solemn as a kiss
The soughing of a silent land.

From the black chasm of the dam
Frogs calling, singular, valiant
Follows the Almighty Quiet.

Oh so quiet
Only rain and frogs, only
Thoughts and breath,
Only love, as sombre and unbreakable
As earth.

Somewhere out there is life,
And mountains
Folded in the bush beyond the hearth
So deeply warmly lit.
There is no answer to the sacred stillness there.

Only a kernel of unanswerable truth.
Does the spirit watch?
Can we grasp the magnitude of these dark tears
Bestowed upon us?
Does night's wing enfold us?
Does it know?

O watchful dark
O watchful broken night
O kiss
O cry
My heart is weighed
With feeling, a heaviness
That no light, no daybreak will redeem
Unmeasurable, implacable as stone –
The granite cliff beyond the rise.

The night, the watchful night,
Cannot undo our doing – but only hold us
In her dark wing as our hearts are trembling
And we can only pray that
We will stumble out alive.

III

Frogs: Ecology of Hope

Deep in winter, stencilled sky
grey up to a russet seam
wetly planted with dark stems.
Mustard riffling, cloud big-lidded
eyes the low vantage point and earth

great anvil, on which day and season
are beaten to sheet metal light.

A child, bow-headed, squats in rushes
in burred flannel, the covert fold of winter's cloth.
marsh, earth, bank and channel
fleshly tongue-textured mud, brown as cattle

Paddocks' far-flung bolt of crabbed corduroy
a sense of fenced pelt.

Child, bent-kneed, boots in soil
lifts dark parcels for gramarye*

See
the brown sternum of rotted wood
flat against ribbed weed,
boned banks flanked by seed rows,
machinery's red flanges and disc-ed fingers.
Strands of mossed fibres break away
roast meat's texture of shank,
grass meshed yellow beneath,
damp humus wet with mould,
swamp-moulded.

---

* Old French for 'magic' or 'necromancy'

Fingers curl beneath the treasured lid:
in that dark purse
pocketfuls

in the hollow haven
bleating jewelly fancies
brown mucus-trembling,
gobfuls of sticky-toffee frogs.
Hold one aloft, a whisper in the hand-

his masterful eye belies the guttural
pelicanese of his fragile-talking throat,
his swallowing moss and bracken backwards
wee frog, brown man, specked priest
in earthen zen coat preaching
'Croak, croak!' he is translating praise.

*

Deep winter-frogs, gumboots, wool, cord,
fires in leaves and grey wool sky, leavened
mohair curled with smoke.
the winter croak, the winter land in winter cloak
and underneath the logs in symmetry
dark earth and mossy tapestry,
the smell of cold – and creatures' precious cant:
small
brown
congregants, found things,
tiled back and lucid eye
membraneous wattling feet,

cool in the palm's crook –
the light stigmata of a kiss-
and the heart in sturdy beat
There, little pebble frog
alive within memory's misty heat,

But where, now?
where art thou, cool damp chorus
beaker click and uvulal vibrato
tremulous crouching throat with knees,
slippery jowl, the body weight of one heavy breath?
Where hast thou fled-
The earth in drought now steep-ed

In space between the land, wood, water and the world
straining the heart's ear to hear
there symphonia amphibia
one in moment
O croak, O jellied spawn
oh once
wherefore?

Bees

Something is killing the bees.
They say that maybe
radio waves have scrambled
their magic radars,
an electromagnetic schism
from mobile phones
tweaking with the instinct
to fly, to pollinate and home.

I wonder
how many people
would give up their
mobile phones
for
honey?

Catholic Schoolyard

Ibis pencil the lawn
near the pencil pines
fat-bodied clerics
syphoning air
they come lilting from the nowhere of sky
disgorged from the red brickwork
from the pale blue Madonna
picking and peopling the quadrangle.

Clawed clefs
forged from iron.
Bow and skewer the earth
with fine sabres
black as filings
Asean, riffling the grass with their beetle extractions.
they are
slightly soiled
manoeuvring
their heavy bottoms behind,
inscrutable grace.

Precisely fashioned,
like a tool
or a gun, pieces fitted into place
utility and art
but quite apart
form following function;
function, form:
stalking the irrigated lands.

*

Ibis in the schoolyard
mimic the lean figures of boys
angled on seats, and leaning
in corners, all elbow and bone
all sharpened face and pencilled eyes
the long Catholic farm boys
awaiting God.

Birds channel absent brothers
bend like nuns
impenetrably clothed in muted tones.

Church bells chime against the sky.

Seahorse Memory

Curled humble thing
floating, finely tooled piece of teak

genus hippocampus
seahorse memory place

wife to husband in
a deep fragile fidelity

in the deep sea of the mind
little seahorse loyal and patient
tender with the memory of the sea's love
bobbing.
mates for life.

Seahorse
knowing, curled together,
long-time longing
and belonging

hippocampus-memory keeper
guardian of the self's own joy and shadow.
The seahorse island in the mind
that little fragile place
that makes me me.

Remember me
Remember
Me
Remember
Seahorse.
Floating.
Falling…gone.

fireflies

at night
the axe of dark
wedged in the hive of hills,
firefly cars dart and bob
up and round, bobbing and weaving
over the rises and culverts
into the stealthy valley, the sharp steeps,
headlights bulging agog
hover over dark streets
light the icy hour
tracing the honey ether behind
home-bound and silent

IV

Diagnos

For Stephanie

The metastatic burning sky…
Here's you flying upside down
into god.
Here from the sky's eye
the delta at dawn
vertiginous: you fall into light
the womb at conception
firestorm from a satellite.
Is that the mind awoken from its sleep
but still shrouded in the fog of dream
the dream of life
yet begun?

'Diagnos' and the following two poems, 'Fallen Small' and 'Boundary Web', were inspired by the paintings of my friend Stephanie Haygarth.

Fallen Small

The fragile rendering
of small things.
As though an awful hand
had dropped them there
bereft, beseeched,
without design.
Broken leaves
and feathers
scattered.
It is the language of southern lands.
It is place –
only the survivors
can testify to its colour and feel.
It speaks quietly
of bush light, and the scent
of eucalypt.
Debris in transcendence,
transient
delicate
as though
the god of small things
revealed through love
the beauty of the whole.

Boundary Web

Clouds flying through blue netting
falling upward in a shroud
light gossamer defiance
scarves' pregnant blue-
bruised blue
teacup and bedding blue
broken petal hue.

Storm
coming and receding
I thought: this boundary web
this netting-full…so fragile
firm and grave:
the cells before division.
the sky through netted eyes.
upward
falling into
love.

Trying Not To Die

I see the rising moon,
the slip rail, sheep run and the dam –
that was where the words began:
the level race, the tufted backs of sheep
and legs in gumboots
up to my ear –

Was I three years old? Bale-high,
my nose up to the grey-boned fence
I looked around
and saw both sheep and sky all roiling into one-
the sheep a frothy tideline through
the drenching run.

'Hup! Hup!' the workers call.
'Hup! Hup! Get around! Goorrrn. Get around
you dog. Hup! Hup! Ooooiiii.'
The waving arms.
Flurry of dust.
The rough chorus 'maaww, maaww'
Of sheep together in the yards.

The farm is within me, even now.

And so, the story goes:
The child wandered, found an old bottle of drenching
chemicals discarded in the dust – some poison, to stop
scouring and worms – and put it in her mouth.
The great hullabaloo.
The young mother horrified with fear, a hospital dash, much
tears, and home again in the afternoon to sob and cuddle

until the day had trailed away into the waiting western sky
the light like lilacs,
as all sunsets flare and die.

'You scared me, then,' she says.
'I was so scared. You scared me.'
But how the fear is shared.

And all those big dark times when she scared me,
And the fear rose like a dust cloud into my heart, and so
fucking scared, I had to flee,
into the vast unknown of broken rock and scree,
and stumbling, scrabbling for the way out of infinity.

You see.

These things are the very heart of who we are –
Those long deep troughs of love and fear,
Home.. and the long spirit shadows
Across the paddocks in the old light of the
Longest afternoon.
My mother, and myself.

And now as we both turn
towards the light, I try to comfort her, as new fears rise
within her dear and fearful breast – so proud and fierce. Lest
we forget, oh lest.

Witness

I remember that first time.
I was so small,
the night folded round the homestead like a dark wing.
down the long years, that evening is recalled

A tableau –
the Last Supper, the long table, the seated few,
the colours in amber and brushed green and dark –
(strange how time embroiders gold on this):
winter teatime, the fire with its warm sound,
there we are floating – in a viscous jar…

from the corner of my eye I see it plain enough:
my little brother struggling. his face bruised and streaked
   with coughing,
my mother, a bulky vision in her big-bellied gown (the
   mound of her fourth child)
rearing into view to sweep him up,
she, shaking him, shouting out an urgent cry…

How slowly we all turned to watch,
how implacably we sensed her fear.
How carefully I watched her face, and realised the deadly stakes
and like an animal I ran
into the dark laundry and shut the door.
And screamed my comprehension to the night.

How slowly does it all unfold, how quickly do we fall…

*

Later we all lay, huddled and chastened by tears
and sobbed and slept
a tumble of bodies in my parents' bed,
my brother quietly in my mother's arms.
She saying 'shhhh, shhhh,'
and, I imagine now,
praying quiet thanks that his small throat had at last disgorged
   the lodged bone.

Such a small wobble of the dice between life and death
such capricious fortune

The farm lay like a black pool beyond the gate – silent,
   watchful,
the sky pinned with scant stars, the lonely distant mawl of
   sheep.
And the breeze that rose at midnight to shush us all to sleep…

Well, all but I –
who lay wide-eyed, and stared into the blackness of the night,
and prayed,
and knew the terror I had seen.
I knew in sudden recognition –
a premonition of the later places I have been.

That was the first time I met Death and, almost witness to his
   crime,
forthwith delayed until another time.

The Tilleys Papers

1

the young waitress
lanky like a boy
blonde fringe covering
her brow down to
her heroin-chic eyes
smudge-black
skinny jeans and gym boots.
in her lunch break she folds
herself onto a stool
shifts the beads of
sadness, beads of lassitude
on her abacus heart

2

young men
in jeans and jumpers, tight beanies and expensive sneakers
half-shaven, slim, intent.
they wait at the bar surrounded by women,
muscular, with quiet poise
a notebook and pen between them,
order strong coffee
planning something big.

3

they walk in separately
through separate doors
she – in a very tidy woollen suit
long red hair like polished hardwood
he nondescript, grey suit, grey hair, air of the Establishment –
tucked in a back booth,
they eat and talk
sip their wine.
nondescript, reserved,
was that a tremor of intent?
and then – a sudden movement in
toward a deep impassioned kiss
open-mouthed, erotic, indiscreet,
broke apart, smiled, and kissed again,
left smiling, conspiratorial
lit from the inside
by a small hot joy.
incongruous and gorgeous.
what a
lunch date!

4 Slavic Matriarchs

On Monday, when the
weather is heavenly,
cool, blue and crystal
with autumn shimmies,
at lunchtime
Slavic women come down the path
to Tilleys,
wheeling prams, Slavic grandmothers,
plain, defiant and unflappable,
harbouring their secrets in
sliding guttural.
While their daughters and
daughters-in-law work, they
are the caretakers of
ancient village rituals
of a lost Europe,
drinking coffee, rocking prams,
feeding toddlers, talking, talking
strong forearms, no easy smiles.
jazz sidles out and the sun warms
the burgundy carpets, glints the windows.
Matrilineal. Blood ties.

5 Writing

Someone is writing by the window
in a foolscap binder – longhand
pages, while he drinks coffee and
in the pauses between ideas and their articulation,
his leg shakes a little – he is unshaven,
but his hand is steady.

6 Staff Pastiche

The girls at the bar are French-looking
and quietly aloof – no chit-chat,
and certainly No Smiles.
and all their black and white uniforms with
little touches of chic, a tie, a waistcoat,
a flower in their hair, or peeping lingerie-
a certain poise and some reserve and a
low reverberating tension – like a secret
untouchable club…a secret burden.

V

Meeting Les Murray

(Sacred Wiradjuri country, Condobolin, 2005)

Out back there, in that far red country,
the land has no description.
It is older than language.
The Language is the Land.
The expression of the Land, is the Land itself: that tussock,
    that rise, that cluster
of grey-green scrub, the jut of earth, that brooding
ooze of rock splashed with the red sun,
those monolithic trees, made of blood and honey, and
    colossal –
Yellowbox and Redgum
Mother Tree and Father Tree…
See yuwaadhuray
spread for miles in the good country, all
gunhanggunhang, yellow-coloured?
Or yarra maranggaal
lining the Lachlan broadly muscled, the earth
gubaagubaa, red of the far west?
Eucalyptus melliodora.
Eucalyptus camaldulensis.
Yuwaadhuray
yarra Maranggaal.
Gunhanggunhang.
Gubaagubaa.
Yellow.
Red.
I see the stain of centuries.

*

Here cometh Yahweh
the Great Patriarch
the Great Murray Grey,
Murray the Grey,
country Gandalf,
brooding beastie
great and noble.
Mr Murray,
from the North Country,
taller and broader than a big tree.
Murray Grey.
Fingers, feet and eyes, more nimble
than dragonflies, dancing mind,
divining ancients while the parochial tumbles behind.

At the lounge room ceremony,
black tea rituals, we sat at his altar
while he yarned, gossipy, sending out
tendrils and missives of words.
'Gossip,' he says, 'the great feral Australian novel
that never ends.' He spake, and, yea, it made sense
and delighted like light-footed minuet
then the suppleness
of willow sapling which femininely bends.
O Great One.

*

Once
simple-hearted boy, with the dark needs of an anointed one,
dangerously brooding and untamed,
ferociously intent, bewildered and
excruciating shy –
such earthly trivia falls away:
when the Poem first came to him, like
a thunderbolt, an answer, from out the sky:

Take this tool, young Dalai, and fashion it to your hand,
fashion a world from it and take a stand.
The Word becometh you, young Murray, and yea,
you shall become the Word.

The boy took the path into the world-
like word to he, so wing to bird.
Bird-like he both noble and ancient, cultured and
primitive – scavenge language, prance, call,
shimmy, build nests of words, soar:
so apprenticed, grew eagle-like, word
his wing and his wind currents.
His spirit blinking out his eyes, he moved
through animalia, absorbing all spirits – bird,
reptile, prowler, fossicker, scuttler,
came into the Proud Bull, beast of pedigree and
rivers, Seer, Patriarch, wizardry and bulk
Sir Murray of the Grey.

*

What shall you say?
All manner of small things
woven into the large, cosmic,
spiritual and heartfelt, an eye for the
prosaic detail that reveals the whole,
the love of the world evoked, the steely eye
extrapolating truths, some malice,
great grace, playfulness and anger,
painterly inside the thought, and deft,
miracle worker
tiny origami of words with great thick fingers,
that agility, dancer, nimble jester
evading, pinpointing, flitting.
Ye shall craft the thought onto the page and the picture
and the sound and heart. Ye shall build the
sweet timbers of the poem, up and out and
together, planing and shaping like a shipbuilder, like a
   woodturner,
melding and bending – tinsmith,
stonemason – carving from the stone block of an idea
or hefty ironmonger, wrenching great steel musculature
of story from out the furnace, fires of life.

For Poetry is an old art, a craft, a Rare Trade, and you may
sit among the artisans and craftsmen and tradesmen
and be a mountain amongst them, and also one of them
and share the old lore of your craft, and learn from them
in their solidity and in their grace, and they from you.

All trades and crafts build the same shape
in its myriad forms and work the same project
together and apart over time, over and over,
the project of Grace and Beauty, the project of creating
truth and balance, the project of God.
And as Jesus, the carpenter, you prefer the company of
such as these, the ordinary man with steady heart
and hands of purpose.
In them sits the crucible of reason, and the path
to enlightenment.
The poet likes to share the bread of these,
and be as a stranger and unknown amongst them.
Tradesman.
Biyaami.

And so, the Great Man came among us
on the rose-coloured day. Condobolin. Condobolin.
The chant of the red and gold land.
Condobolin. Condobolin.
Gunhanggunhang
gubaagubaa
yellow and red –
Blood and Honey Land
and here cameth
Old Man Murray
the Elder of the Tribe
he of the Word.
Of the warm heart, of the sharp eye,
the urge to form.

For Gerard Manley Hopkins

Your tribute to
dappled things, God's honour of imperfect beauty –
windhover, harvest hurrah! Ah!
The freckled girl liked the idea of being 'dappled'.

You used words like some kind
of new joy, like wild music, scatting and pushing
outside the confines of restraint
of your most circumspect of lives, dear Jesuit.
Yet with a deep internal structure that was pure.

I will never forget the tutorial in the back of A.D. Hope
and the smell of books and faded pages,
and the recognition that arose
so suddenly but like a gentle fire – a Christian priest
a hundred years ago, and I, to meet through poetry,
so familiar, so radical, so clear.

Who are you he who spoke to me?

The staunch, defiant rural sensibility
the agrarian ode,
the love for fellow men.
The faith.
The compulsion of the pen.

Your dignity in the service of the poor,
to right the social wrongs.
A humanist priest beholden to
the magnificent misshapen godly glory of the world.

What drove your writing hand?
Love of that Word
that made you
and that made the world.

For Judith Wright

You said you felt you missed your life
from being caught in
gorgeous webs of your imagining,
weaving and beetling
the beautiful ideas.

But Judith –
those webs are how you captured life
its dragonflies and moths,
its bracken and its broken hearts
its blood and sky –
the creeks and hidden ferns, the Budawangs,
the flesh, the truth.

With your
deft and nimble threads.
The silver thread of poems from in your mind
to capture and express
that clear and perfect Life –
dew-spangled, deep, heavy with feeling,

You caught it with your heart
wide open and your pain intact,
your love in equal measure –
of rock and wildy tree
and stumbling humanity.

A passionate captain of the heart
you lived your life, how fiercely
and with what celestial clarity.
You lived and loved and fought and gave
the Goddess of the Land, the Lover, Mother
and with that generous hand, the sacrament was then bestowed,
it showed, that spiritual reality
you did not miss your life.
You lived it – so that poets, women, Nature
could be free.
Two Fires honour thee.

For Kenneth Slessor – Five Bells

Five Bells
you rang for me
when I was twelve years old
and played beneath the apple tree
and hid behind the bike shed
so they wouldn't see.
'Five Bells'

Poet, a picture of you,
showed you in glasses and a tie –
inconspicuous and shy.
But still – the poem that you gave-
It never left me, all my days, electrify
my heart and pierce my mind with
images all watery and lyrical
majestic terrify.
'Five Bells'

In that dusty country school
the empty classroom grey and cool
Five Bells rang through my mind,
the depths of that great pool,
the song to all the delicate undying grace
to all fragility, oh how it haunted me
so beautiful, so cruel.
'Five Bells'

The spirit called me waterly.
It unlocked all the secret fears
the sweet green depths awash with tears
the yearning and the longing of
the gone, the lost and gone
the calling from the distant grave.
I flew with them in dreams
down sunlit years.
'Five Bells'

O great and awful temporality
the beads of gathered light
the water gorging up the awful clarity
poetic charity to one as me
to set me free.
'Five Bells'

For Seamus Heaney

Seamus.
Did you write me, or I you?
From somewhere far away you were so close,
and put your key into my lock,
and turned and set me free
the rural heroism that you lived,
re-lived in me – the old world
forgotten and reclaimed within the new,
O gracious, agrarian, ordinary you.

Plough, hammer, anvil, steel, cogs and lanes, clods and stalls
machines and carts, workshop, smoke…stain…tear.
Only you gave me the
harvest cycles, the handwork
of my father's calloused fingers,
the simple men in working clothes
utilitarian and real
the steady drum beat of those rural lives,
their secrets and their ordinary dreams
their dignity,
their grace,
the tangible humanity of their toil.
Their stoicism.
Their part, their soil.

Things – in perpetuity.
Ritual, spirit, locality.
Parochialism, and work.
The smell of men, the texture of tweed.
Grain and corduroy,
chisel, shovel, plough.

To find the monumental within the plain
the humble, reverential, elegiac, odes to ordinary pain.

Seamus, grand old one, brother, father, son,
bespoke linguist, tool man, trade, you gave it truth and made me dare.
It was you who made the ordinary rare.

For Walt Whitman

Walt
when I first heard your voice
it made me want to be joyous
I wanted that time to be now
the old world of American
industry, philosophy, liberty.
true liberty
Ralph Waldo Emerson and
Henry D. Thoreau –
they were your comrades and
my seers
the noble words so simple and direct
caressed mine ears
the blade of grass
the self unfurled
the yawp of joy from
humble rooftops of the world,
the skin, the sun, the sex and flesh
the politics of working men
of poetry and
solitude
what more could make more sense to hungry me?
of Song of You across a century
in harmony with a song of me –
I wish that all could see
the sheer profound imperative
of your earthy, deeply humanist and visionary creed.
great bearded man in black and white
what would you say to save us from this night?

For Emily Dickinson

not just your words but your life
little woman – to you I have returned a thousand times.

that one could live so quietly and in such
restrained circumspection
and yet write with such defiant
imaginative majesty
so masterly succinct and clear –
one house, one town, no lovers and no crown
just Emily, a pen, and page
the breadth, the wisdom, love and rage.

upon my wall, your words –
about the sacrifice of one beguiled king.

that they had not chosen him,
but he them,
a brave and brokenhearted statement
that years cannot condemn

it turned faith into something else
by swapping them and he
he chose the crucifix and gladly in humility.
this somehow changed me. (Poem 916 Emily Dickinson)

VI

Totem

Eyes hold war in their deep dark
Intelligent, watchful, sad.
Hands that build houses
Write, play chess and fight
And cup my breast and cunt tenderly.
Body tall and still
Poised in defence, contained.
Nonchalant, unhurried, and tired.
Mind like a dark broad river
Deep, thinking in undercurrents.
Voice like chocolate
Broken and aching
Heart like a wounded warrior,
Warm and yearning, honourable.
Spirit of the black bear.

The Departed

She went at the witching hour
In the chilly still while the children slept and dreamt
In the dark on the end of a needle
Fled through eons to Mother's breast.
One gone.
One in a hotel room
With a track and spoon – glorious, mistaken and bereft
And one slung on a silken rope, the rent unpaid and
A baby lost and a perfect face that could not
Redress the empty heart,
And one with a gun (we cannot speak
Of that, gone to her father before she shone)
And one made a spell of death
And filled his head from the magic cauldron
Till his body replete with poison like his mind
Left sadly, behind – an endless well of sadness,
And utter broken-hearted tears,
And one in a garage while the baby slept
And his wife read stories to the older two,
And one overlooking the sea
As quiet and nimble as a minnow
As beautiful and lost
Incanting Ophelia, Sleeping Beauty and Juliet
And everyone was silenced by her
Exquisite eloquence
And broken for all time.
So many more.

The Sewing Room

The sewing room
At the end of the house
At the end of the veranda
The crooked floor
The bolts of cloth
Piled to the ceiling
The filtered light
The smell of dust and oil
The magic of the cloth
The velvet feel
The far-flung threaded mysteries.
The world's in there.
The old machine
The rainy afternoons,
The hushing roar upon the old tin roof.
Cross-legged on the carpet looking up
While my mother worked
The treadle and the needle,
The hum of the old machine
The smell of cloth
The square of muted green world outside the window
Up high.

Wedding Day

For Stephanie and Aaron

The light now is the most golden of them all
Burnished with the glorious melancholy of autumn
Sacred, resplendent and warm.
It kisses down the valley,
The reds and golds of the turning year,
Down and out to the towns in mourning.

The sky is a truly magisterial blue, perfect and
Unblemished, great and solemn like a prayer,
And beyond, a coterie of black clouds
gathering like elders to hold the shining golden day
in their embrace – offering solace
when it feels that all is lost.

The beauty is heavy, a spirit presence – replete in
equanimity, and a great
wave of peace extends itself
into every nook and corner,
every mile, incanting a soothing murmur of
rocks and bees,
small birds and the gentle breeze.

The golden light enjoins us to believe.
To look up from the dreadful broken moment,
from harrow and keening, from sobbing,
wracking grief, amid the river of tears,
amid the deepest sorrow.

To see in the quiet golden beauty of this day
That the earth will turn, and the time will come for sleep,
That the pain will pass, and the night will fall and the stars
Will offer up redemption, offer up a sanctum from despair,
And the sun will rise in honour of you
And warm the earth
Tomorrow and tomorrow again.

Copper-coloured, solemn and still
This most beautiful day, this most beautiful burnished light,
And the offering of so much,
For what else do we have but this, and love?

VII

My Dark Heart

take these pieces of my dark heart
in a certain light they will shine
like shards of blood-coloured glass against the counterpane
of your wrist
on a dull day they may lie
like broken rubble at your feet,
feeding off the weight of sky
if you pick them from the detritus
they may cut your finger
strangely sharp
and issue forth the
red prick of an intimate tear
and fold back layers of
the flesh and pick out the pieces of a prayer
exposed and laid as on an altar

on a quiet afternoon,
shape them together, they will be
like pottery and mirror
mosaic of a fractious future
reforming in the sun, they may shrink
and glitter,
and in the dark they will
swell and coalesce to make
a beating sturdy whole-

you may feed on them
carnivore, apostle
they will be your bread and wine

take them
pieces of my heart
my secret heart:
in a certain light
they may give you something
flawed
something dangerous and real.

Woman

Feel with my womb first
head and heart combined
the idea of desire, the other's heat
and words like tips of tongue
and fire, and my whole
solar plexus, nipples, breastbone,
my lips, my lips, my
womb and then my head
I feel – the want, the want
the culpable restraint
the eyes.

First Blood

I wrote the first in pen
and when the wine was drunk
and stained my lips and teeth
at the black cackle of midnight
I wrote the next in blood –
the bloodstained page
my trembling hands, they freed my heart.

The days in that small room
beneath the trees,
I wrote and smoked and drank and wrote,
I thought – the life that churns in me, yet so remote,
the pen beneath my veins to dig, to twist,
there's gotta be a better way to feel that I exist.
The ritual of the blood, the pen, the word – the miller's grist.
Desist.
Persist.

Just One

One person who is just for me
to listen to my fears, to steady me,
to brace against the world,
make me honest, take my temperature
when I am sick, mock me when I get too serious,
get drunk with me, show me new places
sit in peace and quiet, calm me in my sleep,
be kind to me, hear me, still me,
feed me, protect me from the dark
to keep me safe and let me be myself.
Just one.

Poem about Love

…as for love – the poet in me
needs rebuke –
that seeker of the shape of things
completing circles
making perfect metaphors
and crafting bright conclusions
out of sweet conundrums,
blind delusions.

The poet is reductive
making narratives that fit imagined peaks and curves
making fairy tales from bits and pieces
imagining a whole from one moment, one
hot breath.

Well, it cannot be denied…
the chaos deeper in remains implied.

But Love is not this. It is:
broken thoughts, interspersed through separated moments,
feelings forming out of flawed couplets
that arise from mundanities and
unforeseen faults and faltering
that do not reconcile, that do not rhyme..
lines incomplete,
and imagery that's often ugly, sometimes vast and then replete,
the broad spectrum of discomfort, the bickering and fear
frustration makes odd shapes, and tattered corners –
days and weeks and months that are neither
noble nor poetic…

but it's there in that imperfect harmony –
something deep and dense and firm
jagged angles and supple scaffolds
bending to the winds.
the quiet spoken 'yes',
the valiant 'no'.

Noise! Noise! – timpanis of flesh
and thought-colliding
broken phrases tenuous
uncertain touch and brokenness
repaired a thousand times with
gentle hands, the glue of patience, time's dishonoured dream.

Love is not a poem.

Though a poem often finds itself a way to breathe
amongst the push and shove of
love.

Walking Wild Side

I walked on the wildest side
skating the thin line between life and death
waiting to disappear…
needing to free myself of fear
I sought abjugation, loathing, denial, annihilation.

Defilement is a way to freedom

Where Did the Bad Man Touch You?

Where did the bad man touch you?
There…there…and there…and
somewhere I don't know.
I saw him over the cubicle door…
in the hall…I was looking up a long way.
I saw him at the table…and then
from the water's edge through the film of blood..
and from the bed…and then head down in the dirt..
I still saw him from down there…
I was my own witness…
he smiled at me and held my hand…
then touched me there, and there..
it kinda hurt the most then…all that smiling..
and the kindness, but he tore me good…
I saw him when I was dying…and..
and later when he was crying…
and then some laughing.. and he touched me
there…and sometimes barely at all…
then inside my skull…and against my neck…
hard up against the wall…and he was there
at the blue pulse of my wrists…
and in my guts…
and he pulled my pants away
to see my nakedness and burned me
with his eyes…
and he fed me and I let him…
and I wanted him to touch me gently..
but he pushed too hard…I hit my head..
on the edge of the bath…
and he was there as I hungered…

and touched me…there…and there…
and there…and then
I woke up…and he was gone…
(and you said 'there, there')
and I was still smiling…
and alive.

www.ingramcontent.com/pod-product-compliance
Lightning Source LLC
Chambersburg PA
CBHW070939080526
44589CB00013B/1574